Observations on a 40-Year January Bird Census in Boone County, Nebraska, 1978–2017

Wayne J. Mollhoff

A Nebraska Ornithologists' Union Occasional Paper

Zea Books
Lincoln, Nebraska
2023

ISBN 978-1-60962-301-2   paperback

ISBN 978-1-60962-302-9   ebook

doi:10.32873/unl.dc.zea.1505

Zea Books are published by the University of Nebraska-Lincoln Libraries.

The University of Nebraska does not discriminate based on race, color, ethnicity, national origin, sex, pregnancy, sexual orientation, gender identity, religion, disability, age, genetic information, veteran status, marital status, and/or political affiliation in its programs, activities, or employment.

Nebraska
UNIVERSITY OF
Lincoln

INTRODUCTIONS

After having run several Breeding Bird Survey routes, and participated in several Christmas Bird Counts, I became curious to see what might be found on a winter count under the more tightly controlled parameters of a census, as contrasted with Christmas counts done with variable numbers of observers.

I was first acquainted with the area briefly in 1961, and I returned to work on a ranch there the next year. While working there in 1962, I became acquainted with ranchers up and down the valley. Since 1962, all the owners I knew then have passed on and the ranches have been taken over by their children or newcomers to the area. When I started the count each January, some of the ranchers would stop to greet me. When I drove up in January 2023, 6 years after the count ended, to record the GPS points at each stop, one guy stopped to greet me. He said he remembered me. He didn't look like the 'Dave' I'd become familiar with over the years, and when I asked who he was, he answered that he was Dan, Dave's brother!

The first 14 stops on the route are on the road through the ranch where I worked. Two ranchers gave me permission to check out areas of complex habitat on their land. Each year before I started, I called ahead to touch base with them and ask about the weather and road conditions. One owner was an avid duck hunter and would comment on what the weather had been like and on how it had affected the

arrival of the northern flocks, and how sometimes conditions caused the flocks to completely overfly the area.
Hearing that made me wonder how it might have affected other species as well.

STUDY AREA

The study was conducted in the northwest quadrant of Boone County, beginning in the northwestern-
most township (Township 22N, Range 8W) and con-
tinuing southeast to a point 1.5 miles northwest of
Albion in Township 20N, Range 6W.

GEOMORPHOLOGY

The first 25 stops followed the Beaver Valley road,
which parallels Beaver Creek, and crosses the creek 3
times. The soil in the valley is an alluvium of sand to
sandy loam named the Elsmere-Wann-Loup Associa-
tion (Hammond et al. 1972). The north side of the road
(the Beaver Creek side) was entirely native grass hay
meadows, while the south side of the road was sandy,
hummocky hill dune pasture.

The last 25 stops were in the heavier, more stable soils that developed on the Peorian loess depos-
ited during the Wisconsinan glaciation, the last of the
4 great glacial periods during the 1.8 million years of
the Pleistocene Epoch.

VEGETATION

Prior to occupation by the first European settlers, prairie fires likely restricted any trees to narrow strips along the perennial streams. With the arrival of farmers, tree planting quickly spread. Some old cottonwood groves date back to the Timber Culture Act of 1873 (also termed Timber Claim Act (Hutchinson 1998). Under it homesteaders could claim an additional 160 acres by planting it to trees, a planted area that was eventually reduced to 10 acres (Olson & Naugle 1997). Lawrence Bruner, one of the founders of the Nebraska Ornithologists' Union, made such a claim near the southwest corner of Holt County in 1883-84, and made trips there later to care for the trees. He later reported on the massive changes to local birdlife wrought by the plantings in later years (Bruner 1902).

By the time I started the project, many of these groves were past maturity and provided nest sites for woodpeckers, owls, hawks, eagles, and other species. Many of the groves had also grown up with red cedars as well, providing food and shelter to other species. The total acreage covered by trees was probably stable, as some of the woodlands were removed and others planted. The effect trees had on the birdlife might shift locally from one wooded area to another, but did not have a profound impact overall.

ECOLOGY

The route for the first 15 stops paralleled Beaver
Creek and included several large beaver ponds where
big flocks of ducks overwintered. Under low wind conditions, the ducks streamed up and down the creek
allowing easy counting. Alternatively, with cold, high
wind conditions, the flocks would sit tight, and I could
hear their quacking without actually seeing any of the
birds.

The number of wintering mallards in the area could
seem incredible. In the late afternoon of 16 December
1988, on a Christmas Bird Count, Duane Wolff and I
saw the birds lift off in groups of 50–200 birds to feed
in cornfields several miles away. It took 20 minutes for
them to leave and we counted 50,000+ ducks.

SETTLEMENT

The earliest proven human occupation along the
route was by people of the Folsom Culture. A pri-
vate collector allowed me to photograph two projec-
tile points, one of them broken and re-sharpened, the
other still at full length. He had found them in a poor
sandy field that has long since been returned to grass.

In the mid-1800s, not long before European settlement, the Lakota, Omaha, and Pawnee tribes all vied
for hunting rights in the area. In a running battle between the Lakota and Omahas, Logan Fontenelle, the
Omaha chief, was killed, and a Lakota youth later
named Crazy Horse became a warrior (Marshall 2004).

The first Europeans with plans to settle in the county were a group from Columbus, Platte Co., Nebraska, who arrived on 13 April 1871. They claimed land on which Albion now stands. Business soon followed and by 2 January 1872, a county judge, sheriff, deputy, treasurer and county commissioners were elected (Hutchinson 1998).

METHODS

I ran the count in January each year, and since I was working full time and tied up at least 2 weekends a month, I was restricted to 1 or 2 weekends to run it.

The count was set up similarly to the USGS Breeding Bird Survey routes with 50 stops, ½ mile (800 meters) apart, all birds counted for 3 minutes, with birds counted at one stop not counted again at following stops. This primarily consisted of raptors and ducks moving downwind ahead of me.

Start time was at local sunrise rather than ½ hour before sunrise, due to lack of bird activity noted before sunrise. I recorded the start time, temperature, sky condition, snow cover, wind speed and direction at the start point and periodically during the count as changes were noted. Wind speed was measured with a hand-held anemometer. Birds were identified by sight with binoculars and spotting scope as appropriate. Only birds within ¼ mile (400 meters) were counted.

Habitat information was recorded at each quadrant around the stop, both by vegetation type and patch size. Count points were initially recorded by legal description (township/range/section/quarter section) and later recorded as GPS points.

WEATHER

As might be expected, maximum wind limits for summer BBS routes were often exceeded. Ground-feeding species like longspurs and horned larks were nearly invisible when feeding in harvested cornfields if no snow was present, but might be seen in big flocks along roadsides with deep continuous snow cover.

One year I had to ski to 2 stops due to roads that were closed all winter by snowdrifts. Typical weather conditions included temperatures that ranged from 15° F (–9 °C) at the start to 25° F (–4 °C) at the end, with winds usually 15–25 mph (24-40 kph) throughout. The coldest count was in 1997, with –15° F (–26 °C) at the start and –2° (–17 °C) at the end and with a NW wind blowing at 35–50 mph (56–80 kph) throughout, producing wind chills of –50° F (–46 °C).

Another big difference from BBS counts was the low number of birds seen. Even with a large total number, often more than half of the total was composed of a few large flocks of ducks or blackbirds. Several counts had total bird counts in the range of 225-400 birds, but more than half might have been in only two flocks, and I sometimes drove for several miles in open farm country without seeing any birds at all. At times it made me wish for the 3 minutes to hurry up, or at least see a bird or two to count!

One of the lowest overall counts was the 1984 count. On the night of 24/25 December 1983, a cold front hit with a temperature of –22° F (–30° C) and 25–40 mph (40–64 kph) winds that lasted all night, producing wind chills factors of –64° F (–53° C). In the morning I found the following species lying frozen to death on the ground, in around my neighborhood in Albion: Sharp-shinned hawk, Northern Flicker, American Robin, Purple Finch, and Harris's Sparrow.

In the fall of 1992, I ran the count three times (early and late October, and mid-November) to see how those counts would compare with the usual January count to follow. Both the species composition and numbers found in January 1993 were essentially the same, leading me to conclude that by the time I ran the early counts, the early migrants were gone and the winter migrants had arrived.

At the beginning of the project, it was a 40-mile drive from home to reach the start point. Halfway through the project it changed to 150 miles due to my job change, and one year it was 1200+ miles due to my mobilization to Ft. Bliss (El Paso) Texas, as an Army Reservist during the second Persian Gulf War.

At one stop with unique, complex habitats (open seep springs, open water creek, marsh, dense shrubby thickets, and cattail stands), I spent an additional 45–60 minutes (depending on snow depth) each year to cover all the habitat types.

As may be expected, major habitat changes were noted during the 40 years. Grassland was converted to farmland, small fields were converted to 160-acre center-pivot fields, occupied homesteads were vacated and later bulldozed away. At some stops, farm fences were removed entirely, removing any sheltering plum thickets and leaving only a few clumps of fireweed and giant ragweed. Woodlots were bulldozed out to increase farmable acreage. New cedar windbreaks were planted and matured to produce berries, which attracted flocks of robins and other berry feeders. The critical importance of specific habitat for breeding birds is just as important for the survival wintering species. Even if food is available, some birds can't use it if protective cover from predators is not available, as pointed out by Charles Elton (Elton 1927).

With many species I felt safe in correlating changes from year to year with habitat change or weather events. With species found only in only a few years, or in low numbers (e.g. juncos), or with only a few occurrences (e.g. pintails, wrens, cowbirds), it seemed a random event. With other species I suspect correlation might only be possible on a regional or continental scale such as Christmas Bird Counts.

Finally, in analyzing the results and attempting to explain the findings, I had to conclude that it would have to take into account individual locations and intensity of storm tracks in every direction around the study area. Such detail is possible on a regional level, but when snowfall amounts can vary in an area only a few dozen miles wide, attempts to do so can either seem impossible or drive one to distraction. An example is the single year occurrence of Common Redpolls, but could be applied to other species as well.

DEFINITIONS

Feedlots: in the ranch country, range cattle are typically fed in the morning on open meadows with hay and protein supplements.

Feed yards: in farm country, cattle are fed in enclosed yards of 2-4 acres.

Shelterbelts: windbreaks that were planted by WPA workers during the drought of the 1930s and consisted of 8–10 rows of Siberian elm, cottonwood, locust, ash, hackberry, Russian olive and red cedar. They were usually found along roads in farmland, and many have since been removed to increase farm acreage, especially since the advent of center-pivot irrigation.

Species Accounts

The following 73 species were recorded during the count:

Canada Goose: Found in 9 years, 416 birds, range 2–175, mean 46. On five occasions flocks were seen flying along the creek or resting on adjacent open hay meadows. Once a flock was seen feeding in a cornfield about ½ mile from the creek about noon.

Trumpeter Swan: Found 2 years (2014 and 2016), 1 and 2 birds. These coincided with a report from a rancher years later that they had bred in the area.

Gadwall: 1 year, 2 birds. Found in a location along Beaver Creek with open spring-fed ponds.

American Wigeon: 1 year, 9 birds. Found swimming in a group on the pond mentioned above.

Mallard: 40 years, 40,045 birds, range 13–7491, mean 1001. Found in small to enormous flocks from stop #1 to #15 where the road paralleled the creek and in lesser numbers where it crossed it. On calm days flocks were also found feeding in cornfields up to a mile from the creek.

American Black Duck: 1 bird, 1 year (1989). In flock of mallards on a pond.

Northern Pintail: 2 years, 6 birds, range 1–5. Found with mallards on an open pond.

Green-winged Teal: 16 years, 137 birds, range 1–27, mean 8.5. Found in small groups among mallards.

Lesser Scaup: 1 year, 1 bird. Spotted after being flushed with flock of mallards.

Common Goldeneye: 4 years, 11 birds, range 1–3, mean 4. Found on ponds with other ducks.

Northern Bobwhite: 8 years, 42 birds, range 1–13, mean 5. Bobwhites are normally found in coveys of 6–12. At night they sit in a tight circle with their heads facing out to conserve heat. One spring I found 8 dead birds of a covey that had been buried by a snowdrift and trapped by ice atop the snow, still with their heads facing out.

Wild Turkey: 1 year, 2 birds. Several individuals got permission to stock turkeys about 10 miles northwest of where these birds were found, and was the most probable source of these birds. In more recent times they have almost become pests.

Greater Prairie-chicken: 32 years, 927 birds, range 1–97, mean 30. On 20 January 2005, on a still, frosty morning, I found 8 males displaying on a lek at 32 °F (0 °C). On 25 January 2012, on another still, frosty morning, I again found 8 birds at 32 °F (0 °C) displaying on the same lek.

Ring-necked Pheasant: 37 years, 482 birds, range 1–102, mean 13. Birds were found throughout the route, frequently in moderate numbers in the cattail swamps along Beaver Creek, as well as around feed yards and cornfields.

Rock Pigeon: 30 years, 465 birds, range 1–76, mean 15.5. Found around building sites, usually at livestock feeding operations.

Eurasian Collared-Dove: 6 years (2011–2017), 36 birds, range 1–21, mean 6. Found only where food from human sources was available, either at feed yards or bird feeders.

Killdeer: 2 years, 2 birds. Both were found at the same bridge over Beaver Creek, but 17 years apart.

Wilson's Snipe: 18 years, 26 birds, range 1–3, mean 1.4. Found only in areas of cattails (*Typha latifolia*) and bulrush (*Scirpus sp.*), and dense thickets of willow (*Salix sp.*) and blue false indigo (*Baptisia australis*), areas that were protected from the wind, with numerous seep springs that never froze.

Great Blue Heron: 1 year, 1 bird, flushed from a spot of open water under a bridge over Rae Creek a mile south of Petersburg.

Golden Eagle: 20 years, 24 birds, range 1–4, mean 1.2. All but 2 sightings occurred in the Sandhills part of the route, coinciding with where the most ducks and prairie-chickens were found. On a CBC in that area, I saw one flying low over the water up the creek flush a small flock of mallards, grab one out of the air, take it to the ground and begin plucking pinion feathers from its wings. Last seen in 2006.

Northern Harrier: 25 years, 50 birds, range 1–9, mean 2. Approximately 75% of the sightings were in Sandhills grasslands and marshes, 25% in farmland.

Sharp-shinned Hawk: 6 years, 6 birds. Approximately 75% of the sightings were in dense, mature hardwood/conifer windbreaks near homesteads. The others were in shrubby marshlands near water, both of which hosted a variety of small passerines.

Cooper's Hawk: 4 birds, 4 years. Two sightings were at the same shrubby/swampy site on consecutive years and could have been the same bird. The other sightings were in heavy conifer/hardwood windbreaks near homesteads with feedlots frequented by blackbirds and sparrows.

Northern Goshawk: One bird, one year. Found at an old cottonwood grove with dense undergrowth of red cedars, bordered by Sandhills prairie and with a pond nearby.

Bald Eagle: 36 years, 189 birds, range 1–20, mean 5.25. When I worked on a ranch there in 1962, the owners told me that there 'had always been a pair present in the winter.' Extensive groves of old cottonwoods, open-water creek and ponds that supported huge flocks of ducks provided food for the eagles. Hog farrowing operations outside of the Sandhills area also provided food

when piglets were still-born and discarded on
fields while spreading manure. At one such site
in 2001, I found 3 adult and 11 sub-adult eagles
feeding together on such carrion on one hillside.

Red-tailed Hawk: 39 years, 168 birds, range 1–11,
mean 4.3. Interestingly, but not surprisingly,
the 40% of the stops in the Sandhills portion
produced 72% of those found, while the farmland which had 60% of the stops produced the
remaining 28%. This tells me that the much
more complex native habitats supported a sig-
nificantly higher concentration of the hawks.
Also, mixed in randomly with the 'normal'
red-tails were 25 Harlan's red- tails across 11
years, along with a single Krider's red-tail.

Rough-legged Hawk: 34 years, 79 birds, range 1–6,
mean 2.3. Similar to findings with the red-tails,
native Sandhills grasslands that composed 40%
of the habitat type also produced 73% of the
hawks, while the remaining 60% of the stops
in farmland only supported 27% of the hawks.
Given those numbers, it could be argued that
the Sandhills supported several times the number of birds per unit area than the farmlands.

Ferruginous Hawk: 2 birds, 3 years. Not surprisingly,
all three sightings of this western species were
in the Sandhills. Ross Lock, former nongame
bird biologist, led a group of NGPC biologists
using aerial surveys to locate, monitor and
band the young from 64 nests 1978–1987 in
Box Butte, Kimball, Dawes, and Sioux counties.

Eastern Screech-owl: The two single birds reported in separate years were the result of seeing woodpeckers moving in cottonwood groves and incidentally spotting the owls peering from a cavity.

Great Horned Owl: 10 years, 12 birds, range 1–2, mean 1.2. Seven sightings were on the south side of old cottonwood groves with the owls sitting in the sun. The others were random sightings near open ponds with waterfowl, plus a single sighted at a farmstead with only a few trees, surrounded by open fields.

Long-eared Owl: 2 years, 5 birds, range 1–2. Birds found roosting at mid-morning in a cedar tree at the end of a shelterbelt. Since I have found active nests in the area, I suspect they may have been the same birds or their progeny.

Short-eared Owl: 1 year, 1 bird. Owl was found sitting atop a muskrat lodge in a frozen beaver pond. The site was protected from the wind by surrounding brush.

Belted Kingfisher: 6 years, 8 birds, range 1–2, mean 1.3. All but one of the sightings were made at bridges over Beaver Creek. The exception was seen flying across an open pond.

Red-headed Woodpecker: 1 year, 2 birds. Seen at an occupied farmstead with a few small cottonwoods. It was an adult with a black-headed sub-adult. They may have subsisted to that point on livestock feed or at a bird feeder.

Red-bellied Woodpecker: 8 years, 9 birds, mean 1.1.
Found at 7 sites where large cottonwoods lined
the creek bank. One site had an extensive shelterbelt that protected a farmstead with an active livestock feedlot.

Downy Woodpecker: 28 years, 92 birds, range 1–9,
mean 3.3. This small, common, permanent
resident was found annually 1978–1992, usually at wooded stops in the Sandhills portion of
the route. In the farmland portion it was found
once or twice at only 5 stops located at homesteads in that portion of the route.

Hairy Woodpecker: 17 years, 31 birds, range 1–4,
mean 1.8. All but one of the sightings was in
the Sandhills part of the route which had mature trees large enough to accommodate holes
for nesting and roosting. The single farmland
sighting had only a small box elder where the
bird was spotted, but there was a more extensive windbreak just over the hill where it probably spent most of its time.

Northern Flicker: 26 years, 46 birds, range 1–5, mean
1.8. Approximately 75% of the sightings occurred in the Sandhills, mostly along Beaver Creek where large cottonwoods lined the
banks. The remainder were at old homesteads
with large dying and dead Siberian elm, box elder, and cottonwood trees.

American Kestrel: 31 years, 56 birds, range 1–4, mean
1.8. Birds perched on trees, power lines and

telephone wires in native hay meadows and Sandhills pasture made up 90% of sightings recorded. The remaining 10% were widely scattered across the farmland half of the route. This indicates to me that there must have been a lot more mouse-size prey available in the grasslands.

Merlin: 1 year, 2 birds. The birds were noted at stops on diagonally opposite corners of one section that had complex habitats along Beaver Creek which hosted many small birds including sparrows, blackbirds, and woodpeckers.

Prairie Falcon: 4 years, 5 birds, range 1–2, mean 1.25. Three of the falcons were seen flying over Sandhills grassland, while the other two were in farm land. Given the paucity of reports and the speed at which the birds move, I could not ascertain any real habitat preference other than to regard them as open-country predators.

Northern Shrike: 13 years, 15 birds, range 1–2, mean 1.2. Compared to its summertime congener, the Loggerhead Shrike, which feeds on insects, birds and mammals, the Northern Shrike's only winter food options are birds and mammals. Both species favor shrublands and open spaces to hunt, and on this route were found in open farm fields (50%), open grasslands (38%) and complex shrub, marshes, and open water (12%). While I have often found food cached in the summer, I found no evidence of such behavior in the winter, perhaps because they could not tear open frozen carcasses.

An interesting observation was finding one shrike three consecutive years on the same unremarkable hilltop. It made me suspect it might be the same bird. At another similar site, I found a shrike in two consecutive years.

Blue Jay: 13 years, 18 birds, range 1–4, mean 1.4. Overall numbers were rather stable throughout the project. The birds were found in a wide variety of habitats throughout the route: tree groves and shelterbelts (45%), feedlots (which often included shelterbelts) (17%), rural housing acreages that often included bird feeders (14%), grasslands (10%), creeks (2%), and thickets (2%).

Black-billed Magpie: 19 years, 47 birds, range 1–14, mean 2.5. The birds were found annually 1978-1994, then seen again 2000, 2002, and 2011. This coincides nicely with the West Nile Virus outbreak (Mollhoff 2016), and the release of famphur (Warbex®). The magpies were hit much harder by the pesticide than crows and other species due to their propensity to sit on the backs of cattle and pick out the larvae of bot flies (*Hypoderma* sp.) The species is now found almost exclusively where cattle are not grazed.

American Crow: 38 years, 1269 birds, range 1–202, mean 33.4. It was difficult to understand what was happening with this common large flocking bird. In the first decade (1978-1989) the number of birds per stop averaged 1.85. In the next decade (1988–1997) they averaged 2.4. In the third decade they averaged 6.5, and in the final decade they averaged 2.1 per stop.

The 14 stops in the Sandhills produced 1104 birds, while the 36 stops in farmland only added 365. Both areas had comparable numbers of feed yards, as well as sufficient roost areas. I had expected the numerous cornfields to have more waste grain for food, but instead found fewer birds.

Black-capped Chickadee: 18 years, 98 birds, range 1–6, mean 5.4. The birds were found annually 1978-1993, again in 1996, 1997, 2000, and last in 2002, spanning the time from when they were common until they almost disappeared. This coincides roughly with the magpie population dynamics. They were found in wooded/shrubby areas, especially if there was water present.

They were found consistently in mixed hardwood/red cedar windbreaks. They also seemed partial to homesteads with bird feeders. I suspect that thickets and cedars were important to provide escape from predators.

Horned Lark: 33 years, 3584 birds, range 1–569, mean 108.6. The consistency of this ground feeder in good numbers gave opportunities to speculate on a number of variables.

Years with minimal snow cover meant that few birds would be spotted in harvested grain fields because they were hard to find foraging among the similarly colored cornstalks. Conversely it meant that with almost continuous snow cover, they could be spotted more easily in the crop stubble. On three years with deep snow and/or ice storms accompanied by blizzard conditions prior to the count, at best only a few birds would be found, most likely because most of them had moved out ahead of, or with, the storm.

Stops in the Sandhills grasslands averaged 7.6 birds per stop, while those in the farmlands averaged 87.2. This 11–fold increase led me to believe that the birds preferred to feed on the larger, easier-to-find seeds found on the largely bare ground in grain fields rather than on the smaller grass seeds in the Sandhills.

Cedar Waxwing: 2 years, 51 birds, range 3–48, mean 25. The habits of this notoriously peripatetic species, both during the breeding and non-breeding seasons, have been commented on by studious birders since their discovery. Found at only two sites, both of which had red cedars and open water available.

White-breasted Nuthatch: 20 years, 48 birds, range 1–6, mean 2.4. This permanent resident was found only at wooded stops with hardwood trees that might be mixed with conifers in shelterbelts. They were found at two of the stops in 8 years, sometimes in 2–3 consecutive years, suggesting they might be the same birds or their descendants.

Brown Creeper: 1 bird, 1 year. The site was at a homestead with large cottonwoods, willows and other trees.

Winter Wren: 1 bird, 1 year. Site on Beaver Creek with extensive boggy area with seep springs, shrubs, and cattails, bordered by wet meadows.

Marsh Wren: 2 years (2000 & 2001), 2 birds, same site as the Winter Wren above.

European Starling: 40 years, 1796 birds, range 1–254, mean 44.9. The species exhibits a wintertime dependence on human activities. During the first six years of the project it was found only around residences with livestock feeding operations at sites near the beginning and end of the route. During the following years it spread to other similar sites. When homesteads and feed yards were abandoned, the birds disappeared, only to re-appear as other similar sites were established. A case could be made that human activity constitutes starling habitat, as surely as marshy seep springs define snipe habitat.

American Robin: 19 years, 1199 birds, range 1–376, mean 63.1. During the first 8 years of the project, the birds were found in windbreaks and total numbers reached 50 birds. By 2008–2011, totals reached 198 birds. At the end, totals reached 376 birds annually when a half-mile-long, double-row cedar windbreak matured and produced berries. There was also some variation when more or less precipitation varied the berry corp.

House Sparrow: 30 years, 572 birds, range 1–119,
      mean 19. The birds were found at 18 differ-
      ent stops. Seventeen of the stops were at farm/
      ranch homesteads, 8 of which also had active
      feed yards. A single stop with sparrows that
      was not directly beside a house was within ¼
      mile (400 meters) of a house. A number of the
      stops had flocks of 40–50 birds fly up while I
      was stopped, accounting for the larger numbers
      at those stops.

House Finch: 2 years, 29 birds, range 4–13, mean 14.5.
      The distribution and expansion of the species
      across the state is discussed elsewhere (Sharp
      et al. 2001). As noted therein, the birds were
      first detected as they progressed from town
      to town, most likely as they were noticed by
      feeder watchers. This expansion seemed to oc-
      cur last in the sparsely populated Sandhills.
      During winters some 'pioneers' among them
      may have led the expansion. Since there are
      no towns on the census route, the two sightings
      likely represent this latter type of movement.

Common Redpoll: 1 year, 180 birds in 2 flocks. At the
      time this seemed wildly improbable, but con-
      sidering their absence in the one year and huge
      flocks the next year, I know it can happen. Dur-
      ing the first half of the project, I traveled annu-
      ally to Minnesota to visit family at Christmas.
      While crossing South Dakota, we sometimes
      drove through 'clouds' of the birds that must
      have numbered in the thousands. The birds

on the census route were found in 1986, when due to weather conditions half-hardy species had low numbers, while other species including Rusty Blackbirds were found in higher than usual numbers.

Pine Siskin: 1 year, 1 bird. Habitat included some creek-side shrubs, open flowing water, and large cottonwoods by a ranch house with a feed yard, but with nothing to distinguish it from other similar sites.

American Goldfinch: 14 years, 102 birds, range 1–30, mean 7.3. It was difficult to figure out a pattern to their visits, since they showed up in such small numbers at 2–4 year intervals. To explain this, one would need detailed knowledge of storm tracks at least to the north and west. Perhaps it could be understood better on a regional scale than on a single 50-stop route. The specific habitats I found them in often, but not always, combined homesteads, trees, and thickets. Such habitats also provided protection from both weather and predators. Overall, I would characterize the species as 'erratic.'

Lapland Longspur: 6 years, 50 birds, range 1–39, mean 8.3. One year I found two birds alone. Every other year they were found feeding among flocks of Horned Larks. Identifying one or two among a flock of larks as they moved through broken-over cornstalks was difficult, especially in bad weather.

Snow Bunting: 2 years, 21 birds, range 1–20, mean
    10.5. One found in 2001 and a flock of 20 in
    2017. Irruptive species, occasionally found in
    the area during harsh winters to our north. At
    one site between census stops on a sub-zero day
    with winds gusting 35–50 mph (50–80 kph),
    I saw a mixed flock of tree sparrows and jun-
    cos along with the 20 snow buntings. It was at
    a low spot between two hills which funneled
    the wind across the road. The juncos and spar-
    rows were hugging the ground behind the pro-
    tection of some grass, while the buntings were
    out feeding and bouncing up and down in the
    wind, seemingly enjoying the wind and entirely
    in their own element.

American Tree Sparrow: 37 years, 910 birds, range
    1–146, mean 24.6. The birds were found most
    frequently at stops with thickets and shelter-
    belts. There was a noticeable gap midway,
    from stops 25-31, made up of open fields with
    no trees or weed patches to provide protection
    from the weather or predators. In native grass-
    land stops in the first part of the route, the
    birds fed on the small seeds of native grass. I
    have such a mix beside my driveway that in-
    cludes little bluestem and side-oats grama, and
    often see both the sparrows and juncos feeding
    under the bent-over grass stalks.

Dark-eyed Junco: 25 years, 206 birds, range 1–40,
    mean 8.2. Found in fewer years and lower num-
    bers than tree sparrows and seemed to utilize

the same food sources as the sparrows. They were often found mixed in with the tree sparrows; indeed, I found mixed flocks of the sparrows and juncos 47% of the time, and flocks with only juncos 53% of the time. Early in the project, 1978–1987, the birds were found almost exclusively along a stretch of shelterbelts and homestead windbreaks that remained in place throughout the project and I found an average of 10.4 birds there annually. There followed a ten-year gap when none were found in that stretch. Then during 1995-2017, I found 4.8 birds annually. Their numbers were not only fewer, but their locations were scattered randomly. This could have been partly due to new home sites being built, but even that was not consistent.

Harris's Sparrow: 3 years, 16 birds, range 1–9, mean 5.3. Found in 1979, 1981, and 2011. Birds were found at a low site with cattails beside a hay meadow. Other sites had mixed hardwoods, conifers and open running water. Too few observations to define a pattern.

Song Sparrow: 5 years, 5 birds. The birds were found in 1979, 1985, 2007, 2010, and 2016. Four of the years they were seen at the same stop with the complex habitat of dense cattails, open creek, seep springs and scattered trees. The other sighting was at a stop with open cornfields and a few large fireweed and giant ragweed.

Yellow-headed Blackbird: 1 year, 1 bird. Bird was in a mixed flock of *Icteridae* that included Red-Winged and Brewer's blackbirds, a Great-tailed Grackle, and Brown-headed Cowbirds. The flock was in a stand of dead green ash snags between open water on Beaver Creek and an active feed yard.

Western Meadowlark: 17 years, 79 birds, range 1–14, mean 4.6. Birds were found in open country: 67% in harvested corn or soybean fields, 12.5% in pastures or hay meadows, 8% in feedlots and the remainder in some combination of the above. It was a pleasant surprise to find 4 birds singing at 18 °F (–8 °C) at one stop, and find 5 others singing at 29 °F (–2 °C) at another stop.

Red-winged Blackbird: 26 years, 7805 birds, range 1–870, mean 300. Any birder out during fall migration has seen huge flocks that may seem innumerable. When they settle in for the winter, they must choose places with adequate food for the sizeable flocks. In my census area that equates to feedlots and feed yards where grain is fed to livestock. Broken down by type of operation, feed yards made up 49% of wintering numbers, followed by feed lots with 34%. The remaining 17% were reported in places with trees, thickets and swamps nearby for shelter. Their flocks sometimes included small numbers of other *Icteridae* as well.

Brown-headed Cowbird: 3 years, 18 birds, range 2–12, mean 6. In 1994 two birds were found in a mixed flock of Red-winged and Rusty Black-birds. In 2002, 12 were found mixed with Yellow-headed, Red-winged and Brewer's Blackbirds, as well as a Great-tailed Grackle.

Rusty Blackbird: 9 years, 120 birds, range 1–68, mean 13.3. In five of the nine years they were reported, they were found in mixed flocks of other blackbirds. In all 9 years they were found in wetland sites.

Brewer's Blackbird: 5 years, 25 birds, range 1–14, mean 5.0. In 3 years they were found with other blackbirds; the other 2 years no other blackbirds were present at the sites. All had water available, in creeks or water tanks for cattle.

Great-tailed Grackle: 1 year, 7 birds. The birds were found in mixed flocks that included other *Icteridae* as well.

Northern Cardinal: 2 years, 3 birds, range 1–2. Mean 1.5. Both times the birds were found at sites with mixed pine, red cedar and hardwoods. One of the sites also included a homestead.

REFERENCES CITED

Hammond CL, Mahnke CF, Brown L, Schulte R, Russell W. 1972. *Soil survey of Boone County, Nebraska.* U. S. Department of Agriculture in cooperation with the University of Nebraska Conservation and Survey Division. 79 pp. +32 map plates.

Bruner L. 1902. A comparison of the bird-life found in the Sand-hill region of Holt County in 1883-84 and in 1901. *Proceedings of the Nebraska Ornithologists' Union* 3: 58–63.

Elton CS. 1927. *Animal ecology.* London, England, Sidgwick and Jackson. 209 pp.

Harrington FC. 1979. *Nebraska, a guide to the cornhusker state.* Lincoln NE. University of Nebraska Press. 424 pp.

Kaul RB, Sutherland DM, Rolfmeier SB. 2006. *The flora of Nebraska.* Conservation and Survey Division, School of Natural Resources, Institute of Agriculture and Natural Resources. Lincoln NE. University of Nebraska. 996 pp.

Marshall JM III. 2004. *The journey of Crazy Horse.* New York NY. Viking, Penguin Group (USA) Inc. 310 pp.

Mollhoff WJ. 2016. *The second Nebraska breeding bird atlas.* Lincoln, NE. University of Nebraska State Museum. 304 pp.

Olson JC, Naugle RC. 1997. *The History of Nebraska.* Lincoln NE. University of Nebraska Press. 302 pp.

Sharpe RS, Silcock WR, Jorgensen JG. 2001. *Birds of Nebraska.* Lincoln NE. University of Nebraska Press. 520 pp.

APPENDICES

Plant names used, per Kaul et al. 2006.

ash = green ash: *Fraxinus pennsylvanica*
blue false indigo: *Baptisia australis*
box elder: *Acer negundo*
bulrush: *Scirpus* sp.
cattail: *Typha latifolia*
cedar = eastern redcedar: *Juniperus virginiana*
corn: *Zea mays*
cottonwood: *Populus deltoides*
elm = Siberian elm: *Ulmus pumila*
fireweed: *Kochia scoparia*
giant ragweed: *Ambrosia trifida*
hackberry: *Celtis occidentalis*
little bluestem: *Schizachyrium scoparuim*
locust = honey locust: *Gleditsia triacanthos*
maple = silver maple: *Acer saccharum*
sedges: *Carex* sp.
soybean: *Glycine max*
willow: *Salix* sp.

ABBREVIATIONS

BBS: Breeding Bird Survey
CBC: Christmas Bird Count
GPS: Global Positioning System
NGPC: Nebraska Game and Parks Commission
USGS: United States Geological Survey

ACKNOWLEDGEMENTS

Thanks are extended to the families of Bilse Robinson, Jr. and Warren Wilton for generously making their properties available in pursuit of this project.

www.ingramcontent.com/pod-product-compliance
Lightning Source LLC
Chambersburg PA
CBHW030010040426
42337CB00012BA/725